SWANLEY TO ASHFORD

Vic Mitchell and Keith Smith

MP Middleton Press

Cover picture: Class N15 no. 795 approaches the down platform at Bearsted in 1938, the third coach in its train being a Pullman car. (A.C.Cawston/NRM)

First published January 1995

ISBN 1 873793 45 6

© *Middleton Press 1994*

Design - Deborah Goodridge

Published by Middleton Press
Easebourne Lane
Midhurst
West Sussex
GU29 9AZ
Tel: (0730) 813169
(From 16 April 1995 - (01730) 813169)

Printed & bound by Biddles Ltd,
Guildford and Kings Lynn

CONTENTS

ACKNOWLEDGEMENTS

We are grateful to those mentioned in the photographic credits for the assistance received. We would also like to express our gratitude to D.Allard R.Airey, P.G.Barnes, R.M.Casserley, G.Croughton, F.Hornby, J.B.Horne, P.Horne, J.R.W.Kirkby, S.Lamb, A.Ll.Lambert, N.Langridge, Rev.H.Mace, R.Randell, Mr.D. &.Dr S.Salter and our ever helpful wives.

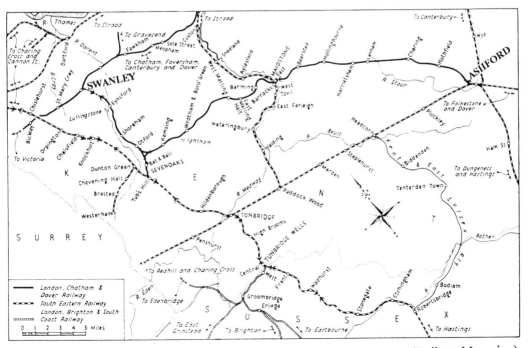

(Railway Magazine)

GEOGRAPHICAL SETTING

From Swanley the route runs south for two miles on the Chalk of the North Downs, passing through the highest part in a tunnel. It enters the Darent Valley at Eynsford and continues close to the north-flowing River Darent as far as the junction with the Sevenoaks branch. This climbs onto the sand of the Hythe Beds on which the town is situated.

The main line runs east between the steep scarp slope of the North Downs and the high ground of the Hythe Beds. It is on the latter from West Malling to Maidstone where it dips steeply in to and out of the Medway Valley. Thereafter the line was built predominantly on the Gault Clay at the foot of the North Downs as far as Hothfield. From there the route descends onto Wealden Clay near the old established market town of Ashford, which is situated at the confluence of the Great Stour and East Stour Rivers.

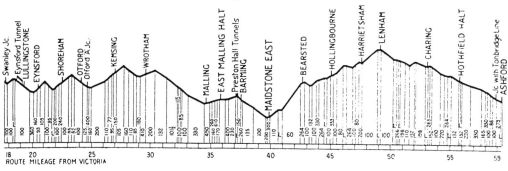

HISTORICAL BACKGROUND

The South Eastern Railway completed its Redhill-Ashford main line in 1842 and extended it to Folkestone the following year. A branch north from Paddock Wood to Maidstone came into use in 1844. The SER's North Kent Line was extended south from Strood to link with this branch at Maidstone in 1856.

Into this area of SER monopoly came the London, Chatham and Dover Railway with its main line from Rochester to London on 3rd December 1860. A branch south from this route via Shoreham became Sevenoaks first railway, opening to the present Bat & Ball station on 2nd June 1862. Built by the Sevenoaks Railway, the line was absorbed by LCDR in 1879. The SER provided Sevenoaks with a station at Tubs Hill on 2nd March 1868 when its Chislehurst branch was extended there, preparatory to linking with the main line at Tonbridge on 1st May 1868. The Sevenoaks Railway linked the two stations on 1st August 1869. The LCDR worked all trains on the branch from the outset.

The LCDR extended east from Otford Junction to Maidstone on 1st June 1874 and on to its own station at Ashford on 1st July 1884. Thus the SER had a competitor in all the major towns of the district. The rivalry ended on 1st January 1899 after which date the two companies were united under a joint managing committee, the system soon becoming known as the South Eastern & Chatham Railway.

The railways of the area became part of the Southern Railway on 1st January 1923 and were nationalised on 1st January 1948 to become part of British Railways. Electrification took place as follows -

Swanley - Sevenoaks	6 January 1935
Otford - Maidstone East	2 July 1939
Maidstone East - Ashford	9 October 1961

The Tonbridge line had for long been designated Boat Train Route 1, the Maidstone East route being BTR2. They continued to be so described as steps were made to upgrade them for Channel Tunnel traffic in 1994.

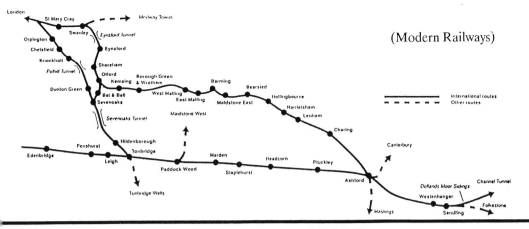

(Modern Railways)

International routes
Other routes

PASSENGER SERVICES

The following summary refers to down trains from London and omits trains running on less than five days per week.

By 1869 Sevenoaks was receiving eight weekday and five Sunday trains. The 1876 timetable showed 12 and 6 respectively with the line to Maidstone having 7 and 6. Following the completion of a triangular junction south of Otford on 1st November 1880, all Maidstone trains from Swanley ran via Sevenoaks, reversing at the present Bat & Ball station. A local service operated between the two Sevenoaks stations.

The 1885 weekday service comprised nine trains to Sevenoaks, six of these reversing and continuing to Ashford. On Sundays, three terminated at Ashford, one at Maidstone and two at Sevenoaks. Most trains conveyed Victoria and City portions, joining and dividing taking place at Herne Hill.

Following a financial disagreement between the LCDR and the SER, passenger services between Bat & Ball and Tubs Hill were suspended from 1st July 1886 until 31st December 1898.

No regular services used the northern part of the triangular junction until 1st January 1899, after which date only one train each way reversed at Sevenoaks (Bat & Ball), a shuttle service being provided between Otford and Sevenoaks (Tubs Hill).

This ran until 1st January 1917 when it was discontinued as a wartime economy measure. An unadvertised train ran on Saturday evenings in 1918 but it did not call at Bat & Ball. At this time there were four trains terminating at Maidstone and ten at Ashford, all but one calling at all stations. The Sunday figures were two and four respectively. The shuttle recommenced on 1st March 1919.

Electrification between Swanley and Sevenoaks in 1935 brought a 20-minute weekday interval service (giving 52 trains daily) and role reversal at Otford whereby it became the starting point for most of the local trains to Maidstone East. This station received 19 weekday trains at that time, eleven of which continued eastwards, the proportion being similar on Sundays when electric trains were half-hourly to Sevenoaks.

The introduction of electric services to Maidstone East in 1939 gave an hourly train from Victoria to Swanley where it divided for Gillingham and Maidstone East. Including peak hour extras, there were 22 weekday trains at this time. An hourly steam-operated connection to Ashford was provided. The Sevenoaks service was reduced to half-hourly in 1958.

Electrification of the remainder of the route in 1961 resulted in two Ashford trains per hour, one stopping at Swanley, Otford then all stations and the other running fast from St.Mary Cray to Borough Green calling thence at Maidstone East, Bearsted, Lenham and Charing. From July 1967 the former terminated at Maidstone East and the latter called at all stations east thereof. May 1970 brought a reduction to one train per hour east of Otford, calling at all stations. Two trains per hour were restored to the Ashford route in May 1988 when Sevenoaks began to receive Thameslink trains from stations north of London. These originated at Blackfriars from May 1994.

Since May 1989, Maidstone East has had the benefit of three trains per hour with the addition of an express from London, next stop Ashford.

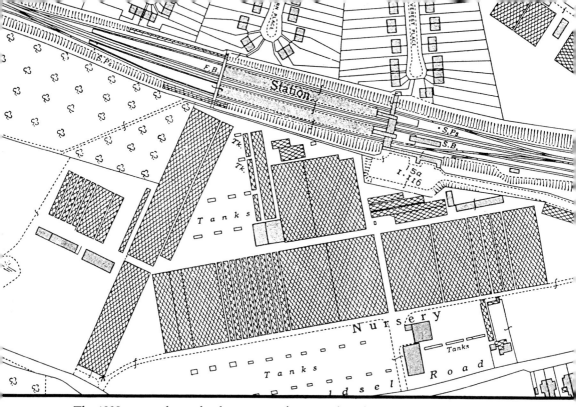

The 1939 survey shows the then new station on the left, its predecessor having been at the divergence of the lines. Those to Rochester are on the right, the Sevenoaks tracks being lower right. This and the next map have been reduced to about 20" to 1 mile. Note the strategic position of the jam factory close to the junction of two lines from the Garden of England. The siding, bottom right (on the up side) was electrified for berthing.

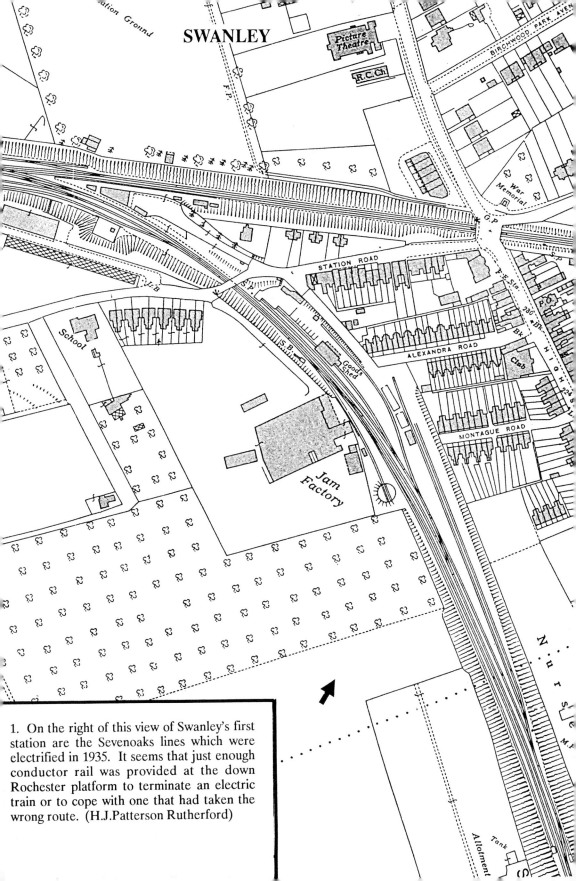

SWANLEY

1. On the right of this view of Swanley's first station are the Sevenoaks lines which were electrified in 1935. It seems that just enough conductor rail was provided at the down Rochester platform to terminate an electric train or to cope with one that had taken the wrong route. (H.J.Patterson Rutherford)

2. The approach road to the original station is shown on the map. The name "Sevenoaks Junction" was used from its opening on 1st July 1862 until 1st January 1871 when it became "Swanley Junction". The new station was called simply "Swanley", the name being in use from 16th April 1939. (Rev.A.W.V.Mace)

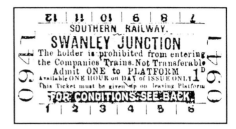

3. The Sevenoaks platforms are seen from the footbridge shortly before electrification. Also evident is the water tank which supplied columns at the appropriate end of each platform. A locomotive has propelled two coaches on the down line under the road bridge, which was rebuilt in 1994. (H.J.Patterson Rutherford)

4. A brazier stands by the water column as H class 0-4-4T no. 1264 waits with an up train from Maidstone East. The guard's look-out on the leading coach gave this type the nickname "Birdcage". (D.Cullum coll.)

5. The 6.23pm from Holborn Viaduct arrives behind class B1 4-4-0 no. 1450 on 28th June 1937, bound for Gillingham. The siding in which is standing class E no. 1175 had been the scene of a serious collision on the previous day. Note the length of this platform and the position of the signal box. (H.C.Casserley)

Earlier maps and other pictures of this station can be seen in the companion album *Bromley South to Rochester.*

6. In order to facilitate the dividing and joining of electric trains, a new four-platform station was built in 1938-39. A new signal box (left) controlled the repositioned signals from 31st May 1939. Compare this picture with the previous one to assess the increase in cutting width. (National Railway Museum)

7. The wagons in the previous picture are standing on the berthing siding shown on the right of this one. There was access to it from both ends. After World War II the 3 SUB electric units were augmented with one wider steel-bodied coach, evident here. The doorway (centre) once served the porters room. (H.C.Casserley)

8. An eastward view in 1992 shows a bridge for a public footpath and a covered bridge for passengers, the small booking hall being at its southern end. Numbered from the right, 1 and 3 are for up trains. Until June 1959, 1 and 2 were up platforms. All were lengthened and colour light signals introduced at that time. (J.Scrace)

9. The junction layout was altered in 1959 in association with revised working of the quadruple track east of Bickley. Unit no. 1574 forms the 13.11 from Victoria to Ramsgate on 19th January 1993. The junction has been controlled by Victoria Panel since 19th June 1983. (M.Turvey)

SOUTH OF SWANLEY

10. The goods shed and part of the yard are included in this record of nos. 31246, 31545 and 31727 pausing on 25th February 1961 on their way from Feltham to Ashford for scrapping. The yard closed on 16th May 1964 but Swanley Yard Box had ceased to function on 19th May 1939. (J.J.Smith)

May's sidings were ¾ mile south of the junction and were shown on the 1896 survey and this 1938 edition.

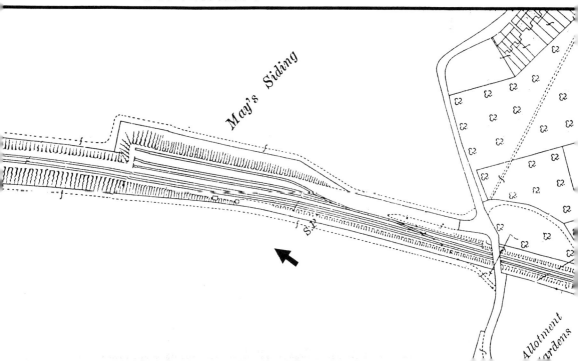

LULLINGSTONE

This map at 3" to 1 mile has Swanley Junction at the top, Eynsford station at the bottom and the 828yd. long Eynsford Tunnel in the centre. Also shown is the proposed airport and branch thereto, planned in 1937.

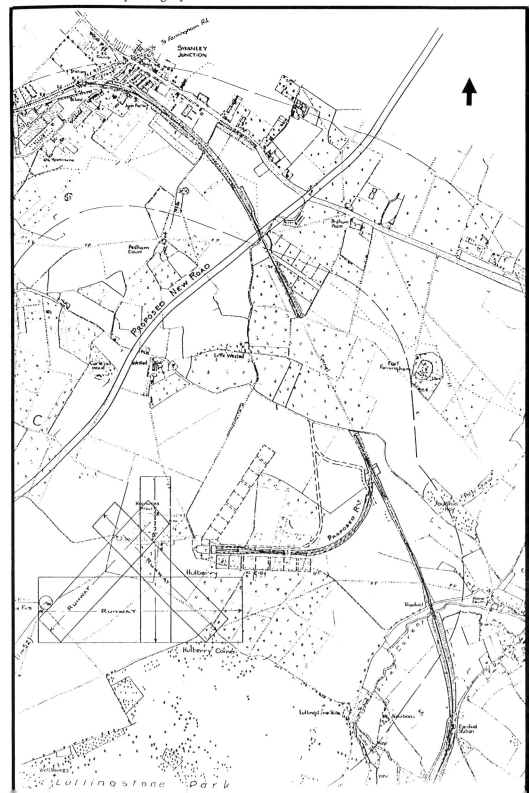

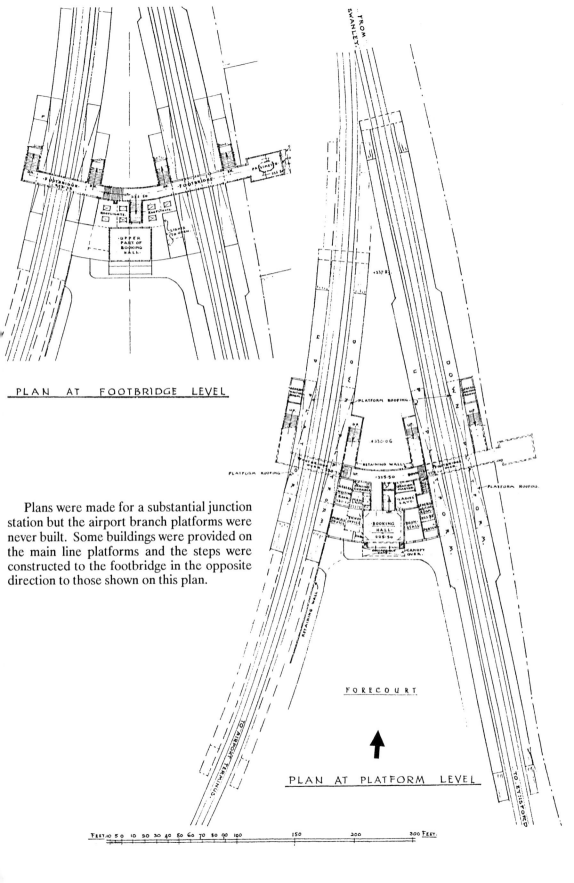

PLAN AT FOOTBRIDGE LEVEL

Plans were made for a substantial junction station but the airport branch platforms were never built. Some buildings were provided on the main line platforms and the steps were constructed to the footbridge in the opposite direction to those shown on this plan.

FORECOURT

PLAN AT PLATFORM LEVEL

FEET 10 5 0   10   20 30 40 50 60 70 80 90 100   150   200   300 FEET.

11. Two photographs from 5th March 1955 show the unopened station being demolished. This northward view includes the straight bore of Eynsford Tunnel. The platform canopies had been removed for reuse at Canterbury East but the platform facings could still be seen in place in 1994. (S.C.Nash)

→

Hourly departure times appeared in public timetables from May 1939 until October 1941! Thereafter and until June 1954 the name continued to be shown. This handbill is from 1939. Even the Ordnance Survey indicated the station as open on its 1940 edition of the 1" scale map.

12. A southward panorama from the footbridge includes Eynsford in the distance. The anticipated housing development on the 5000-acre Lullingstone Estate (purchased by Kemp Town Brewery Co.) had not taken place and after World War II "Green Belt" legislation prevented it. The brewery had paid towards the cost of the station. (S.C.Nash)

SOUTHERN RAILWAY

EVERY SUNDAY,
MAY 7th to JUNE 25th, inclusive,
EXCURSION TO
BRIGHTON & LEWES

DEPART.		FROM	RETURN FARES, Third Class, TO :—	
All Dates.	May 28th to June 25th, inclusive.		LEWES	BRIGHTON
a.m.	a.m.		s. d.	s. d.
—	10A 9	ST. MARY CRAY*		
—	10A14	SWANLEY*		
—	10A17	LULLINGSTONE	4/2	4/9
—	10A19	EYNSFORD*		
—	10A24	SHOREHAM (Kent)*	4/2	4/2
—	10A27	OTFORD*		
—	10A30	SEVENOAKS (B. & B.)	3/8	4/2
9B29	10B56	SEVENOAKS (T.H.)*	2/8	3/8
9 55	11 38	TONBRIDGE	2/8	3/8
10 5	11 52	TUNBRIDGE WELLS CENTRAL	2/1	3/2
	p.m.			
10 10	12 2	TUNBRIDGE WELLS WEST* ...	2/1	3/2
10 19	—	GROOMBRIDGE*	2/1	2/8
10 25	—	ERIDGE*	1/7	2/8
10 34	—	CROWBOROUGH*	1/7	2/1
10 44	—	BUXTED	1/4	1/7
10 51	—	UCKFIELD*	1/1	1/7

Arrive		At	
11 8	12 40	Lewes	**CHILDREN, 3 TO 14 YEARS, HALF-FARE.**
11 26	12 57	Brighton	

RETURN TIMES, SAME DAY :—

FROM	Train No. 1 All dates.	Train No. 2. May 28th, to June 25th, inclusive.	Arrive about	Train No. 1. All dates.	Train No. 2. May 28th to June 25th, Inclusive.	Arrive about	Train No. 1. All Dates except May 7th, 14th & 21st.
	p.m.	p.m.		p.m.	p.m.		
BRIGHTON	7 55	8 48	UCKFIELD	8 27	9 24	SEVENOAKS (B. & B.)	10A41
LEWES ...	8 12	9 6	BUXTED	8 34	9 29		
			CROWBOROUGH ...	8 45	9 39	OTFORD ...	10A44
			ERIDGE	8 54	9 46	SHOREHAM(Kent)	10A47
			GROOMBRIDGE ...	8 59	9 51	EYNSFORD ...	10A52
			TUN. WELLS WEST	9 6	9 58	LULLINGSTONE	10A54
			TUN. WELLS CENT.	9 19	10 16	SWANLEY ...	10A59
			TONBRIDGE ...	9 28	10 25	ST. MARY CRAY	11A 4
			SEVENOAKS (T.H.)	10B19	—		

A—Change at Sevenoaks (T.H.) and Tonbridge.
B—Change at Tonbridge.

THE SOUTHDOWN MOTOR SERVICES LTD. run Special Motor Tours to many places of interest in the neighbourhood.
Tickets obtainable in advance at Stations and at the Offices of Messrs. Baldwin's Travel Agency and Pickford's Ltd. at Tunbridge Wells

NOTICE AS TO CONDITIONS.—These tickets are issued at less than the ordinary fares and are subject to the Notice and Conditions shown in the current Time Tables.
No luggage allowed except small handbags, luncheon baskets or other small articles intended for the passenger's personal use during the day.
On the RETURN journey passengers may take with them, free of charge, at Owner's Risk, goods not exceeding in the aggregate 60 lbs. which they may have purchased for their own use (not for sale).
DOGS, BICYCLES and PERAMBULATORS.—Reduced rates for return journey. FOLDED MAIL CARTS conveyed free.

Waterloo Station, S.E.1.
March, 1939.

GILBERT S. SZLUMPER,
General Manager.

C.X. 482/11/23339   38337

Printed in Great Britain by
McCorquodale & Co. Ltd., London.

13. The nine 30ft arches of Eynsford Viaduct carry the line at a height of 70ft. above the River Darent and the lane to Lullingstone Roman Villa. An up freight is about to tackle the 1 in 100 up gradient which continues through the tunnel. The tranquil scene was recorded in the 1930s. (Rev.A.W.V.Mace)

EYNSFORD

The 1896 survey indicates only two sidings and a wagon turntable. The station opened on 1st July 1862.

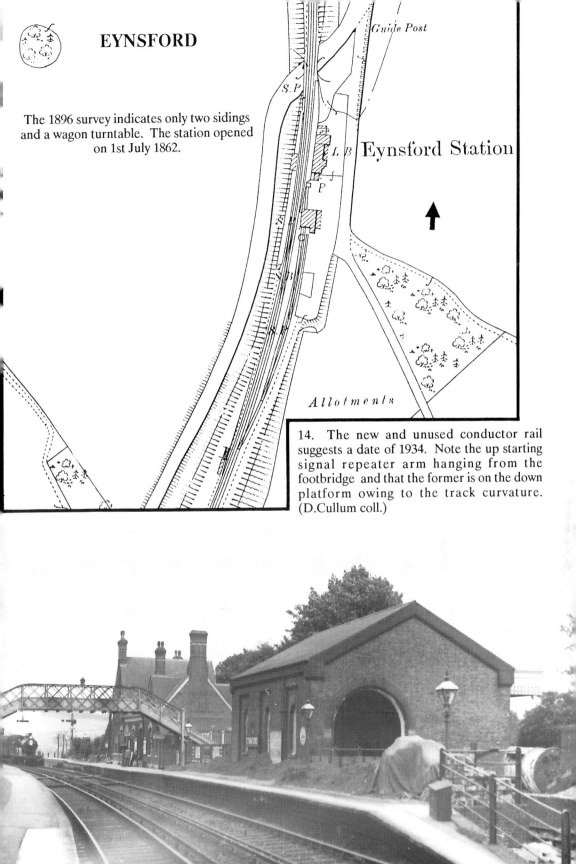

Guide Post

S.P.

L.B   Eynsford Station

P

Allotments

14. The new and unused conductor rail suggests a date of 1934. Note the up starting signal repeater arm hanging from the footbridge and that the former is on the down platform owing to the track curvature. (D.Cullum coll.)

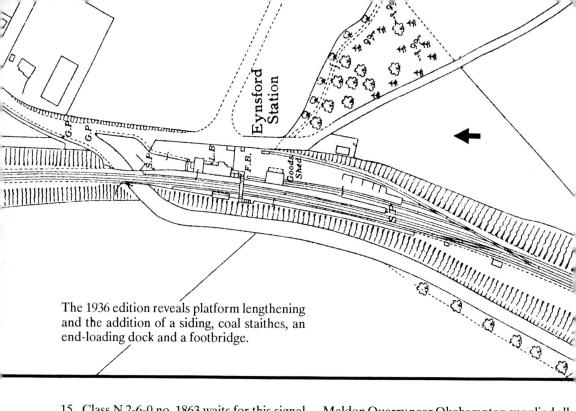

Eynsford Station

The 1936 edition reveals platform lengthening and the addition of a siding, coal staithes, an end-loading dock and a footbridge.

15. Class N 2-6-0 no. 1863 waits for this signal to clear on 24th February 1934. Its load would be used for reballasting in Eynsford Tunnel. Meldon Quarry near Okehampton supplied all of the stone used by the SR at that time. (H.C.Casserley)

16. The awkward 50-chain curvature is evident in this southward view from August 1954. The bay window of the booking office housed the signal frame which was in use from 9th November 1932 until 21st February 1971. (D.Cullum)

17. A 1970 photograph features the concrete footbridge which replaced the original lattice structure. It is formed from standard SR pre-cast components but with an unusual reverse flight on the down platform. The goods yard (right) had closed on 7th May 1962. (J.Scrace)

18. The station is well situated for motorists using the A 225 but in the pre-motor age it was inconvenient for the village, being a half mile from its centre. The east elevation presented a smart appearance in October 1992. (J.Scrace)

19. A novel time is indicated as the 13.22 Ashford to Victoria departs on 10th April 1994. By then the station was staffed only on weekday mornings. (M.J.Stretton)

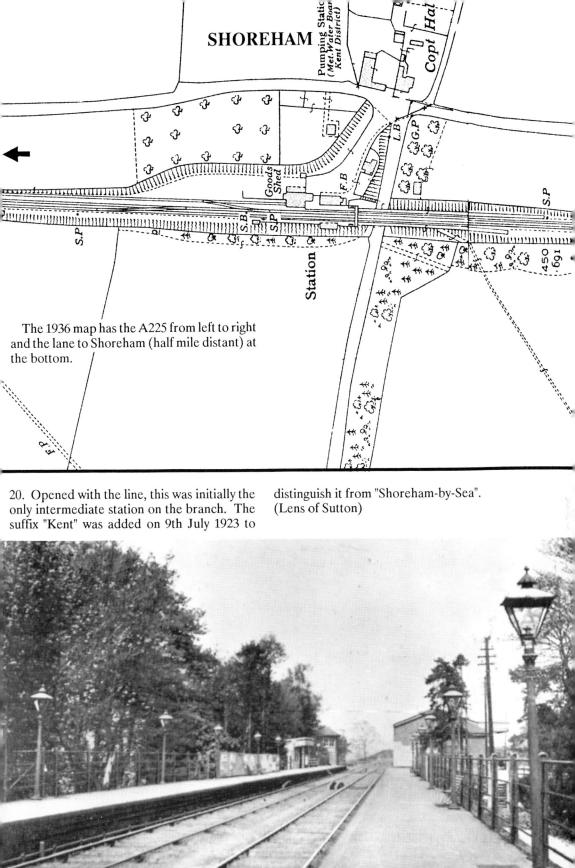

SHOREHAM

The 1936 map has the A225 from left to right and the lane to Shoreham (half mile distant) at the bottom.

20. Opened with the line, this was initially the only intermediate station on the branch. The suffix "Kent" was added on 9th July 1923 to distinguish it from "Shoreham-by-Sea". (Lens of Sutton)

21. A "Schools" class locomotive speeds past the small buildings on a gloomy day in January 1956. The footbridge had been completed in 1935 in readiness for electrification. (E.Wilmshurst)

22. The east elevation in 1968 includes the well-aerated partially roofless gentlemen's toilet. The village population was 1250 when the line opened and increased by only 250 in the following 60 years. (British Rail)

23. The goods yard closed on 7th May 1962 but Ashby Bros maintained their coal business on the premises, seen in 1968. The goods shed continued to be used for joinery production more than 30 years after its closure. (British Rail)

24. The crossover and headshunt are included in this 1970 record of the signal box which closed on 21st February 1971, when colour light signals were introduced. (J.Scrace)

25.   A 1992 photograph includes part of Otford's canopy which had been added to the section of the building that had been used as a Countryside Centre since 1986. Staffing of the booking office ceased on 18th July 1992. (J.Scrace)

26. The 10.49 Victoria to Ashford arrives on 13th October 1992, a service still worked with guards. On the opposite platform are tele-vision cameras and monitors used by drivers of Sevenoaks trains which are devoid of guards. (J.Scrace)

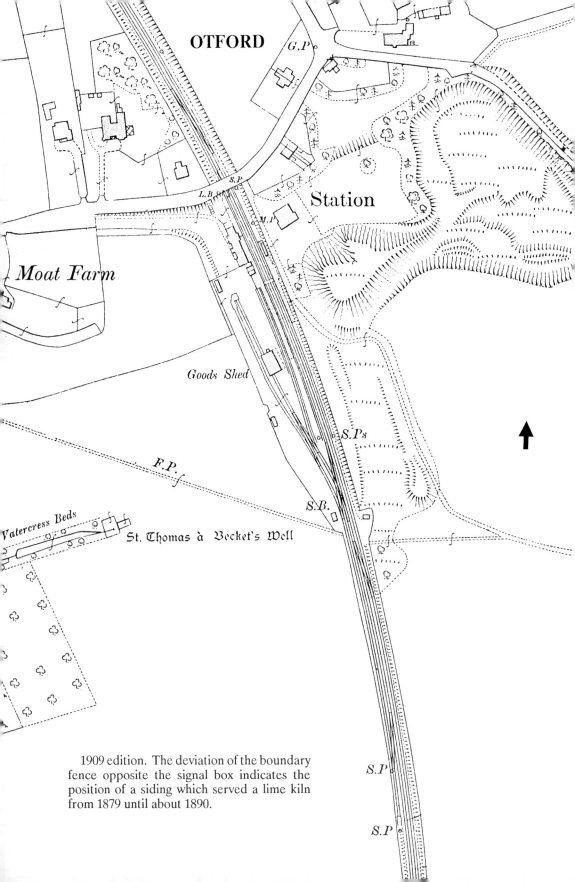

OTFORD

G.P

Station

Moat Farm

Goods Shed

F.P.

S.Ps

S.B.

Vatercress Beds

St. Thomas à Becket's Well

S.P

S.P

1909 edition. The deviation of the boundary
fence opposite the signal box indicates the
position of a siding which served a lime kiln
from 1879 until about 1890.

27. Otford station opened on 1st August 1882. By 1902, a covered footbridge lengthened platforms and generous canopies had been added. New signs in 1904 reflected its importance as a junction station for Sevenoaks, and the name reverted to "Otford" on 7th July 1929. Photographed here in about 1912 we see a traction engine and trailer belonging to nearby Castle Farm. (E.Thompson coll.)

28. Pictured in January 1913 is Station Master H.T.Willis who was in office here from 1900 until 1915. In the background is an oast house, on the left is the Sevenoaks bay and in the foreground is some unusual ballasting. Gas replaced oil lighting in 1911. (E.Thompson coll.)

29. Also recorded in January 1913 were the signal box and staff. The 35-lever frame was in use until 19th July 1970 having controlled an additional up line from Otford Junction since 11th March 1962 when some colour light signals came into use. The up loop was taken out of use on 19th February 1970 but remained as a trailing siding. (E.Thompson coll.)

30. The push-pull coaches of the Sevenoaks shuttle stand in the bay platform in 1922, with the upper arm of the coacting up starting signal silhouetted against the sky. The population of Otford rose from 804 in 1861 to 2295 in 1921. (H.J.Patterson Rutherford)

31. Three six-wheeled ex-LCDR coaches and an ex-SECR P class 0-6-0T formed the Sevenoaks train on 3rd April 1926 and for many years previously. The engine is now on the Bluebell Railway. R class 0-4-4Ts were introduced in 1927, displaced by ex-LBSCR class D1 0-4-2Ts from 1929 and returned in 1931, being used until electrification. (H.C.Casserley)

32. Class J 0-6-4T no. 1599 departs for Maidstone East in 1934. Two crossovers to the siding in the foreground gave run-round facilities when required. The hut behind the train was for signal & telegraph staff. From 1935 to 1939 most Maidstone services started from the bay. (Rev.A.W.V.Mace)

33. The peaceful station car park and vegetable allotments were recorded in August 1954. Upon electrification in 1935, the number of weekday trains to London increased from 20 to 54 and Sunday services from 11 to 34. (D.Cullum)

34. The complex trackwork in front of the signal box, the water column and part of the goods yard were photographed on 28th August 1954. The latter closed on 7th May 1962. (D.Cullum)

35. The 13.02 Bedford to Sevenoaks service arrives on 16th March 1994 formed of Thameslink dual-voltage class 319 units. In May of that year they were superseded by class 465 Kent Networker trains. Most of the building was in commercial use at that time but the booking office was still staffed. (M.Turvey)

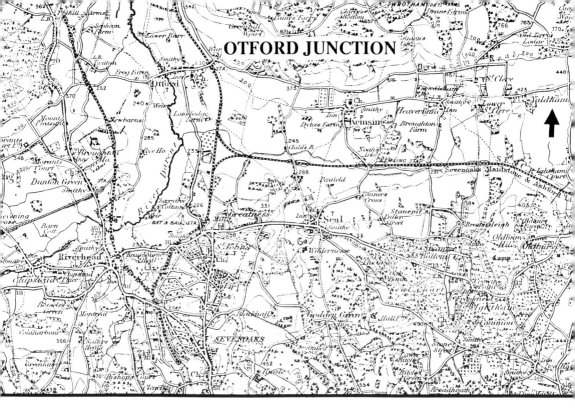

OTFORD JUNCTION

The 1912 map at 1" to 1 mile has Sevenoaks at the bottom and the two routes from London at the top. The original Otford Junction station was situated at the northern apex of the triangular junction and was in use from 1st June 1874 until 1st November 1880. It was used solely for exchange purposes, there being no road access, much to the frustration of the residents of Otford.

This sketch was made from a surviving plan dated 1874 . The Sevenoaks line had been doubled by 1st August 1863 while the Maidstone route was still single. This was doubled between Wrotham and Malling by 1881 and completed by 1st July 1882. The bridge on the left is shown on the 1" scale map and X marks the approximate position of the later junction. The site is now traversed by the M26.

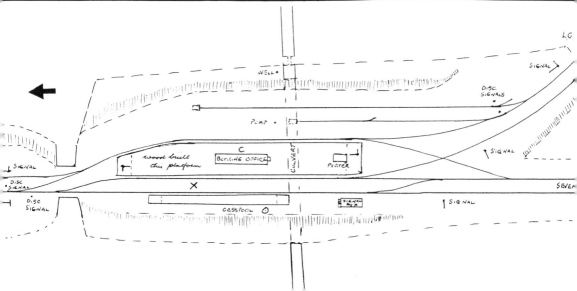

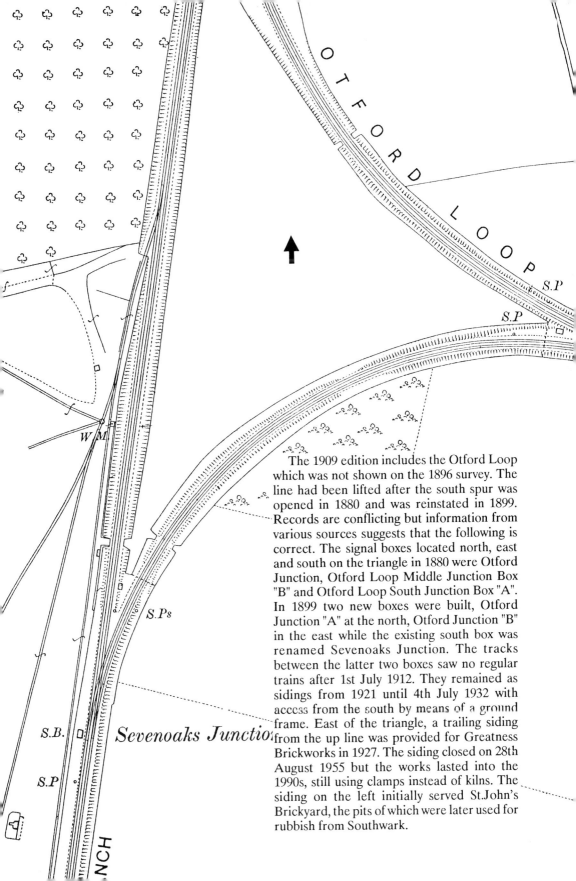

OTFORD LOOP

S.P

S.P

f

W M

S.Ps

S.B.

S.P

Sevenoaks Junction

NCH

The 1909 edition includes the Otford Loop which was not shown on the 1896 survey. The line had been lifted after the south spur was opened in 1880 and was reinstated in 1899. Records are conflicting but information from various sources suggests that the following is correct. The signal boxes located north, east and south on the triangle in 1880 were Otford Junction, Otford Loop Middle Junction Box "B" and Otford Loop South Junction Box "A". In 1899 two new boxes were built, Otford Junction "A" at the north, Otford Junction "B" in the east while the existing south box was renamed Sevenoaks Junction. The tracks between the latter two boxes saw no regular trains after 1st July 1912. They remained as sidings from 1921 until 4th July 1932 with access from the south by means of a ground frame. East of the triangle, a trailing siding from the up line was provided for Greatness Brickworks in 1927. The siding closed on 28th August 1955 but the works lasted into the 1990s, still using clamps instead of kilns. The siding on the left initially served St.John's Brickyard, the pits of which were later used for rubbish from Southwark.

36. Unit no. 5135 is working the 10.20 Holborn Viaduct to Sevenoaks on 2nd April 1970. These 4EPBs served the route well until displaced in 1988. The severe 19-chain curve of the Maidstone route begins in the foreground, this having a 30mph speed limit. (J.Scrace)

37. Photographed in 1979, the box then controlled the route from Shoreham to Bat & Ball and an engineers siding at Otford. The box closed on 5th June 1983 when Victoria Panel took control of the area east to Kemsing. (British Rail)

38. Nuclear flasks from Dungeness to Willesden Brent normally travel via Tonbridge but on 13th January 1994 this train was diverted, due to a landslip. No. 33008 is approaching Otford Junction from Maidstone East and is passing the site of Greatness Brickworks siding where a new passing loop was being built for use when required by Channel Tunnel traffic. (C.Wilson)

BAT & BALL

The 1909 survey includes the long 1902 private siding to the premises of the Sevenoaks Gas Company. The part in Crampton's Road was laid in granite setts and single wagons were hauled by two horses, later displaced by a Fordson tractor. In 1914, 9760 tons of coal were conveyed over the line. The South Suburban Gas Co. took control in 1932 and production ceased on 9th September 1960. Later editions show the 1934 siding for the Kent Sand & Ballast Company trailing from the up line near the bottom left corner of the map. Part of it, including its points were still in situ in 1994.

Tank

F.P.

CRAMPTON'S ROAD

W.M.

7a

TRAMWAY

S.P.

F.P.

S.P.

S.P.

Brewery

S.P.

Sig.

Cattle Pen

Goods Shed

Coal Depot

Bat & Ball Station

S.P.

S.P.

W.M.

CHATHAM HILL RD.

S.P.

C.R.

S.E. & C.R.

BRANCH

39. A 1921 panorama of the North Downs from Otford Road bridge includes the gasworks siding curving behind the water tower (left) the engine shed (right) and the water column in the foreground. Note that there were starting signals at both ends of both platforms. (H.J.Patterson Rutherford)

40. The turntable was situated between the engine shed and the station building and was obscured by the former in the previous picture. Designed by Martley, LCDR no. 34 was for some time named *Herald* and was of the "Dawn" class. It became SECR no. 493 and was withdrawn in 1904. (E.Thompson coll.)

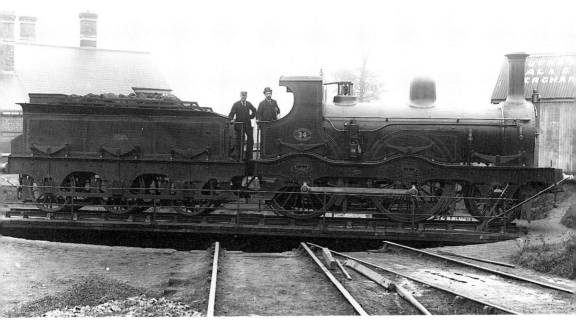

41. The goods shed, signal box and approaching passenger's view were recorded in April 1963. Coal wagons are in the goods yard which closed on 25th March 1968, having been a coal depot only since 18th April 1966. A new road now passes very close to the station and the other buildings have been demolished. (British Rail)

42. The interior was photographed in 1967 and provides a record of conditions in a typical country or suburban station of the period, although most had lost their gas lights by then. The tiny slotted ticket window is on the right. (British Rail)

43. On the left is the two-part stable-type door seen on the right of the previous picture. A small shelf was provided on the top of the lower one on which to stand parcels. Note the racks for Edmonson card tickets, the dial-less telephones, the string-repaired chair and that some modernisation had come in the form of mechanised accounting. (British Rail)

44. "Sevenoaks" was dropped from the station name on 5th June 1950. The use of "and" or "&" has been inconsistent. The signal box remained in use until 22nd November 1981 and was photographed in August 1970. (J.Scrace)

45. Most of the early platform buildings remained in place when the 11.00 Luton to Sevenoaks train was photographed on 13th October 1992. Station staffing had ceased on 1st June of that year. (J.Scrace)

SEVENOAKS BRANCH.

WEEK DAYS.

DOWN.

		1	2	3	4	5	6	7	8	9
		Gds.	Empt	A	A	A	A Gds.	A	A	
M.		a.m.	a.m.	a.m.	a.m.	p.m.	p.m.	p.m.	p.m.	p.m.
	Swanley .... arr.	...	...	8 45	11 29	1 49	1 30	5 16	6 25	...
	Swanley .... dep.	6 40	...	8 46	11 30	1 50	2 0	5 17	7 13	9 50
	May's Siding .... „	...	...	...	...	...	2 8	...	...	...
3	Eynesford .... „	6 55	...	8 53	11 37	1 57	2 25	5 24	7 20	9 57
5	Shoreham .... „	7 10	...	9 0	11 43	2 3	2 42	5 30	7 26	10 3
...	Robertson's Siding ...... „	...	...	...	...	...	2 52	...	...	...
8	Sevenoaks (Bat & Ball) „	7 20	8 35	9 9	11 50	2 12	3 0	5 39	7 33	10 10
...	Sevenoaks (Tub's Hill) arr.	...	8 39	9 13	11 54	2 16	...	5 43	7 37	10 14

UP.

		Gds.	A	A	A	A	A	A Gds.		Empt	
M.		a.m.	a.m.	a.m.	p.m.	p.m.	p.m.	p.m.		p.m.	p.m.
	Sevenoaks (Tub's Hill) dep.	...	8 53	9 45	12 12	3 53	6 45	...		9 20	10 20
	Sevenoaks (Bat & Ball) „	6 0	8 57	9 49	12 16	3 57	6 49	7 30		9 24	10 24
	Shoreham .... „	...	9 4	9 56	12 23	4 4	6 56	7 50		9 31	...
3	Eynesford .... „	...	9 10	10 2	12 29	4 10	7 2	8 5		9 37	...
5	Swanley .... arr.	6 20	9 17	10 8	12 35	4 16	7 8	8 15		9 43	...
8	Swanley .... dep.	...	9 18	10 9	12 50	4 17	7 9	8 45		...	...

SUNDAYS.

DOWN.

	1	2	3	4	5	6	7	8
	Eng.	Empt			Eng.	A		
	a.m.	a.m.	a.m.	a.m.	p.m.	p.m.	p.m.	p.m.
Swanley .... arr.	7 25	...	...	...	...	6 18	...	...
Swanley .... dep.	7 26	...	9 51	11 38	...	6 19	7 22	10 25
Eynesford .... „	...	...	9 58	11 45	...	6 26	7 29	10 32
Shoreham .... „	...	...	10 4	11 51	...	6 32	7 35	10 38
Sevenoaks (Bat & Ball) „	7 45	8 5	10 11	11 58	6 20	6 41	7 42	10 45
Sevenoaks (Tub's Hill) arr.	...	8 9	10 15	12 2	6 24	6 45	7 46	10 49

UP.

			Eng.		A		Empt	Eng.
	a.m.	a.m.	p.m.	p.m.	p.m.	p.m.	p.m.	p.m.
Sevenoaks (Tub's Hill) dep.	8 25	10 53	12 10	6 40	8 30	9 50	10 55	...
Sevenoaks (Bat & Ball) „	8 29	10 57	12 14	6 44	8 34	9 54	10 58	11 0
Shoreham .... „	8 36	11 4	...	6 51	8 41	10 1	...	...
Eynesford .... „	8 42	11 10	...	6 57	8 47	10 7	...	...
Swanley .... arr.	8 48	11 17	...	7 4	8 53	10 14	11 17	...
Swanley .... dep.	...	...	...	...	8 54	...	11 18	...

A These Trains run through between London and Sevenoaks.

Trains not stopping at Swanley must run through that Station very slowly

L. C. & D. Trains must carry, between Bat & Ball and Tub's Hill Stations, Sevenoaks, one White Disc by day, and one Green Light by night, on smoke box.

L. C. & D. Down Trains must give Two Whistles on approaching the junction with the S. E. R., and Up Trains must give Two Whistles when starting from the Station.

Working timetable for January 1871.
Eynsford was spelt with one "e" in the public timetable. The suffix "Bat & Ball" was added on 1st August 1869.

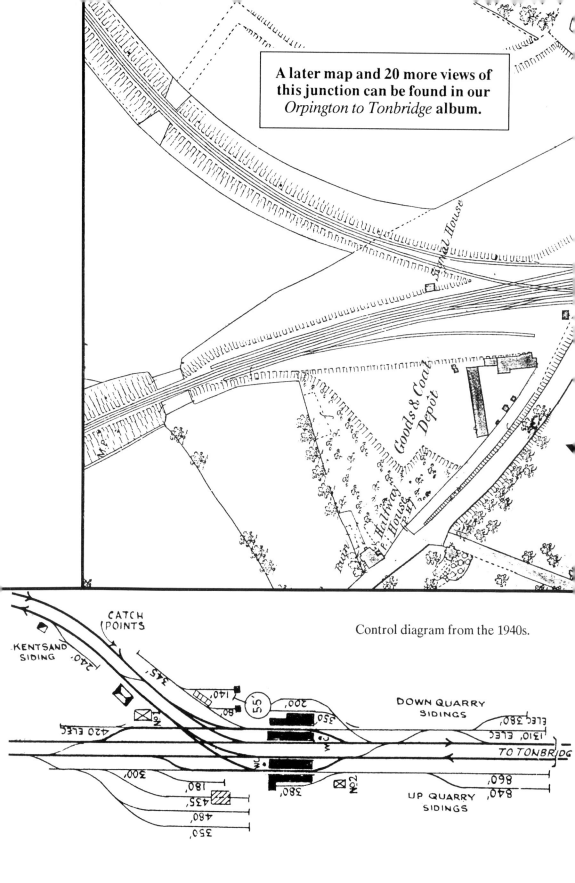

A later map and 20 more views of this junction can be found in our *Orpington to Tonbridge* album.

Signal House

Goods & Coal Depot

Halfway House

M P

CATCH POINTS

KENTSAND SIDING

240'

345'

140'

80'

55'

200'

350'

420 ELEC

No1

No3

W.C.

No2

300'

180'

435'

480'

350'

380'

Control diagram from the 1940s.

DOWN QUARRY SIDINGS

ELEC 380'

1310' ELEC

TO TONBRIDGE

860'

840'

UP QUARRY SIDINGS

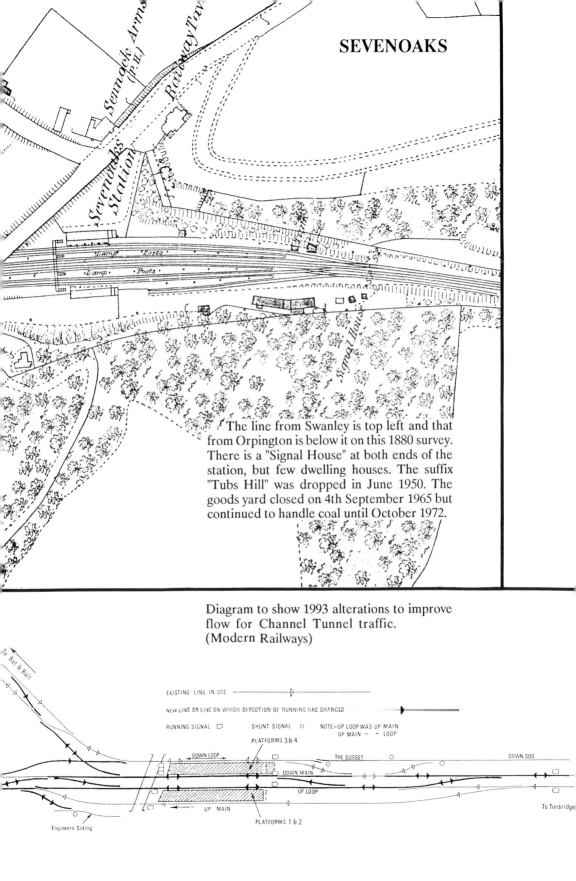

SEVENOAKS

The line from Swanley is top left and that from Orpington is below it on this 1880 survey. There is a "Signal House" at both ends of the station, but few dwelling houses. The suffix "Tubs Hill" was dropped in June 1950. The goods yard closed on 4th September 1965 but continued to handle coal until October 1972.

Diagram to show 1993 alterations to improve flow for Channel Tunnel traffic.
(Modern Railways)

EXISTING LINE IN USE

NEW LINE OR LINE ON WHICH DIRECTION OF RUNNING HAS CHANGED

RUNNING SIGNAL   □   SHUNT SIGNAL   ○   NOTE:-UP LOOP WAS UP MAIN
                                              UP MAIN " " LOOP

To Bat & Ball

PLATFORMS 3 & 4

DOWN LOOP

THE GUSSET

DOWN SDG

DOWN MAIN

UP LOOP

UP MAIN

To Tonbridge

PLATFORMS 1 & 2

Engineers Siding

46.   A group of musicians hurry to join a Tonbridge train as the subject of our interest stands on the turntable road in 1926. P class no. 178 was used on the Otford shuttle from the recommencement of service on 1st February 1919 and was sold from the BR fleet in 1958 to Bowaters & Lloyds Ltd. Like its sisters nos. 27 and 323, it is now on the Bluebell Railway. (Rev.A.W.V.Mace)

47.   No. 323 was relief engine for no. 178 when it required a boiler wash-out or other maintenance. The station had four through lines but six platform faces, the "Otford Motor" usually using the eastern pair. The station was completely rebuilt in 1976. (Lens of Sutton)

48.   Sevenoaks "A" Box was in the vee of the junction and closed on 4th March 1962. Its all-electric successor was in use until 28th June 1993 when Ashford Panel took over. Mr. William Stupples holds the traditional signalman's cloth. (G.Anckorn)

KEMSING

49.   Two photographs from 23rd April 1938 fully illustrate the small station which served under 1000 residents, most of whom lived at least one mile distant. This includes the 3.44pm Maidstone East to Victoria and the signal box, which closed on 30th September 1964. (H.C.Casserley)

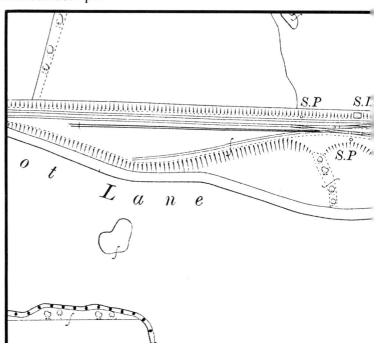

50. The 2.34pm Victoria to Ashford, hauled by J class 0-6-4T no. 1597, passes the small goods yard which was in use until 31st October 1960. The only significant change here was the provision of a concrete footbridge at the east end prior to electrification. (H.C.Casserley)

Lower right is one of the Sevenoaks Water Work's pumping stations which would have required a coal supply. This is the 1909 edition. Staffing ceased on 8th February 1985 and the buildings were demolished shortly afterwards.

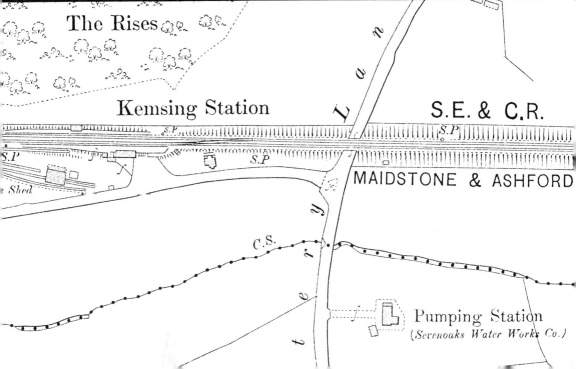

The Rises

Kemsing Station

S.E. & C.R.

MAIDSTONE & ASHFORD

Pumping Station
(Sevenoaks Water Works Co.)

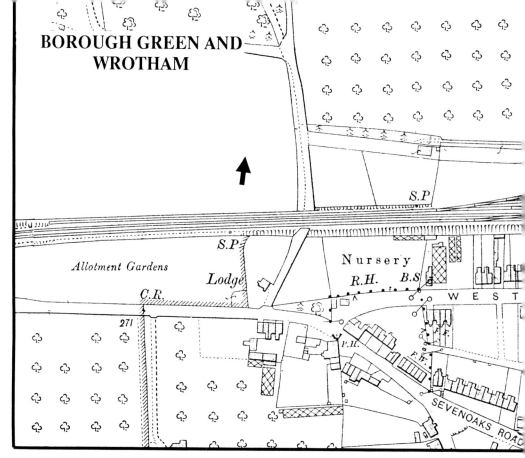

BOROUGH GREEN AND WROTHAM

Allotment Gardens

C.R.

271

S.P

S.P

Lodge

Nursery

R.H.   B.S

WEST

P.H.

SEVENOAKS ROAD

51. A view from the road bridge in about 1934 includes the dock siding and the 5-ton capacity goods crane. Only small cranes in the goods sheds were available at the other stations betwen Swanley and West Malling inclusive. (Rev.A.W.V.Mace)

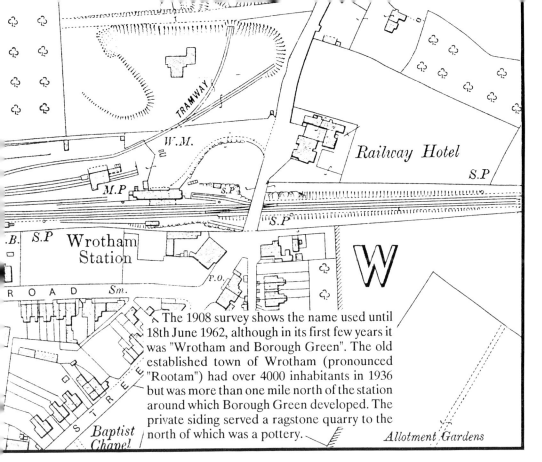

Wrotham Station

The 1908 survey shows the name used until 18th June 1962, although in its first few years it was "Wrotham and Borough Green". The old established town of Wrotham (pronounced "Rootam") had over 4000 inhabitants in 1936 but was more than one mile north of the station around which Borough Green developed. The private siding served a ragstone quarry to the north of which was a pottery.

52. Surplus train heating steam issues from the rear coach of the 1.48pm Saturdays-only Holborn Viaduct to Maidstone East, which was headed by ex LSWR class T9 4-4-0 no. 300 on 23rd April 1938. (H.C.Casserley)

53.   On the same day class C 0-6-0 no. 1590 runs in the opposite direction with a van train. The prolific blossom adds to the beauty of the locality each April. (H.C.Casserley)

54. The architecture reflects the importance of Wrotham, although its population was under 4000 when the railway arrived. Its potential for goods traffic, notably fruit and vegetables, was shown by the size of its goods yard, but this closed on 9th September 1968. (C.Hall)

55. The Southern Electric Group's rail tour on 13th April 1991 used preserved 4SUB no. 5001, affectionately known as the "Green Goddess". The footbridge was erected prior to electrification and obscures the down electrified loop that was added in 1961 to increase line capacity. It was relaid and extended west in 1994 for use in connection with international traffic. (A.Dasi-Sutton)

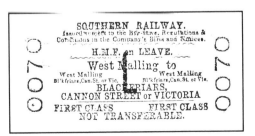

SOUTHERN RAILWAY.
Issued subject to the Bye-laws, Regulations &
Conditions in the Company's Bills and Notices.
H.M.F. on LEAVE.
West Malling to
West Malling   West Malling
Bl'kfriars,Can.St. or Vic.   Bl'kfriars,Can.St. or Vic.
BLACKFRIARS,
CANNON STREET or VICTORIA
FIRST CLASS   FIRST CLASS
NOT TRANSFERABLE.

56. Pascall's (at one time Spencer's) private siding was on the down side near Platt. Passing it on 13th May 1956 is Schools class no. 30934 *St. Lawrence* with the diverted 4.20pm Sundays - only Margate to Charing Cross. (S.C.Nash)

57. Mrs Rose Reynolds is pictured here at Offham Crossing in August 1968. She had been resident keeper here for 42 years and had witnessed the closure of the public siding (on the up side) on 5th September 1961. The crossing closed on 10th November 1969 when the road was diverted to use an adjacent underbridge. (E.Thompson coll.)

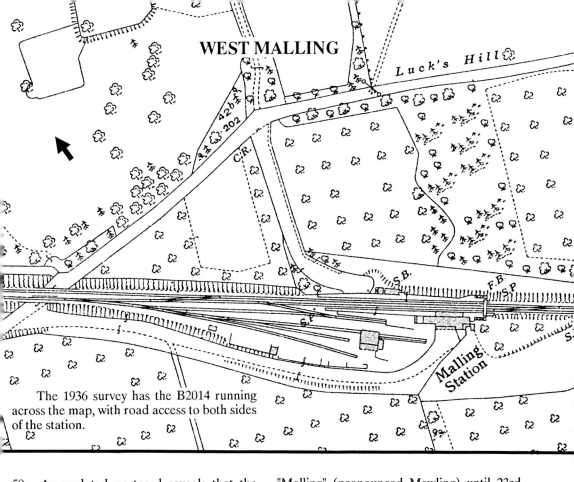

WEST MALLING

Luck's Hill

Malling Station

The 1936 survey has the B2014 running across the map, with road access to both sides of the station.

58. An undated postcard reveals that the footbridge was there in the days of ground-length skirts. The station was named simply "Malling" (pronounced Mawling) until 23rd May 1949. (Lens of Sutton)

59. The south facade was a mirror image of its westerly neighbour and was photographed in 1970. The population of West Malling was over 2000 when the line was built. (J.Scrace)

60. The signal box, also recorded in 1970, continued to control semaphore signals until its closure on 9th December 1983. Opposite, on the up platform, was a large store for bicycles. (J.Scrace)

61. In the civilised pre-juggernaut days, electric locomotive no. E5008 moves a large tonnage of freight almost silently from Hither Green to Dover on 2nd April 1970. It may have been more costly but a good quality environment has to be paid for. (J.Scrace)

62. A 1982 westward view shows that the waiting shelter adjacent to the signal box had been modernised but that the once-busy goods yard had been overwhelmed by the trees on the left. It had closed on 19th May 1964. (D.Cullum)

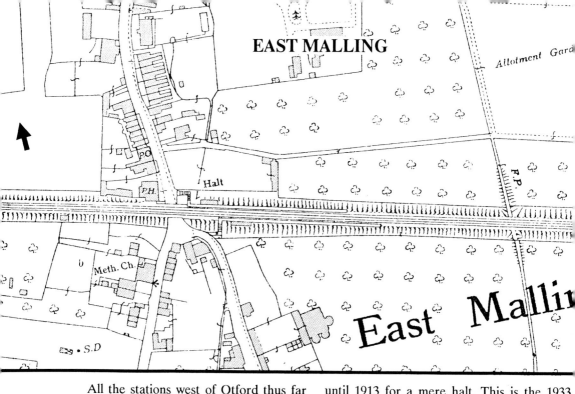

Allotment Gard

Halt

P.H.

P.O.

Meth. Ch.

.S.D

P.P.

East Malli

All the stations west of Otford thus far opened with the line on 1st June 1874 but the 2000 or so residents of East Malling had to wait until 1913 for a mere halt. This is the 1933 survey.

63. This is the up side, where the wooden steps were at a right angle to the track. The halt was surrounded by orchards, the dwellings being generally scattered. (Lens of Sutton)

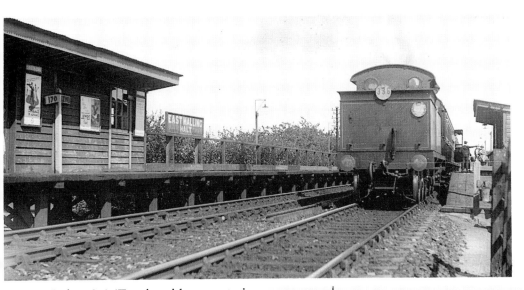

64. A J class 0-6-4T waits with an up train while the guard gives directions to some ladies. A horticultural research station and the Ditton Laboratory were nearby. Only five locomotives of this class were built, all in 1913. (Lens of Sutton)

65. Empty stock passes through on the down line on 3rd August 1993. The waiting shelter was new but the timber platforms had been replaced by concrete slabs in the late 1950s. (J.Scrace)

About one mile east of the halt, a quarry siding was provided, it being shown here on the 1932 edition. It was then operated by Eggleton and Cochrane. East of this were the two short Preston Hall Tunnels (33 and 54 yds long), created for the benefit of the landowner. They have recently been eliminated.

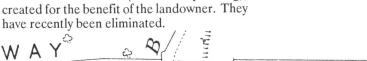

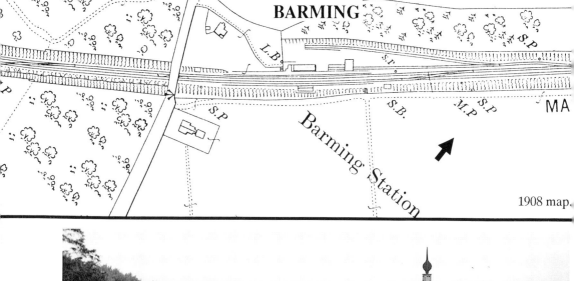

BARMING

L.B.

S.P.

S.B.

M.P.

S.P.

MA

Barming Station

1908 map.

66. A 1916 photograph conveys well the rural situation of this station, most of the 1000 residents being at least one mile to the south. The line drops at 1 in 135 and 100 from here into the Medway Valley. (Lens of Sutton)

BARMING

67. With a backdrop of hop poles, the signal box was photographed in May 1971. It remained in use until 24th April 1982 when colour lights were introduced. (J.Scrace)

68. A Maidstone East to Victoria service approaches the station on 8th April 1967, comprised of two 2-coach units. The goods yard had been to the left of them and had been in use until 5th December 1960. (J.N.Faulkner)

69. Seen on 3rd March 1990, 4VEP no. 3471 reaches the end of the 60-chain curve into the station. A right-hand curve of 36-chain severity for ½ mile takes trains down to the Medway bridge. (R.Palmer)

MAIDSTONE EAST

The 1908 map has the ex-SER line and the River Medway from top to bottom and our route from Swanley on the left. The ground rises steeply from the river to the east so the station had to be built on a restricted site before the line enters Week Street tunnel, (right) which is 98 yds in length. It is followed by Wheeler Street tunnel, 358 yds in length. The short down siding left of centre has a small platform with a footbridge connecting to the corn mill. This siding was electrified for berthing in 1939. The sidings close to the words *STREET WARD* were laid down in 1882 by the Midland Railway to serve their coal depot. Their successors (the LMSR) sold the site in 1934 but it continued to be used for coal. Goods traffic ceased on 13th September 1965. The crane (Cr.) was of 10-ton capacity.

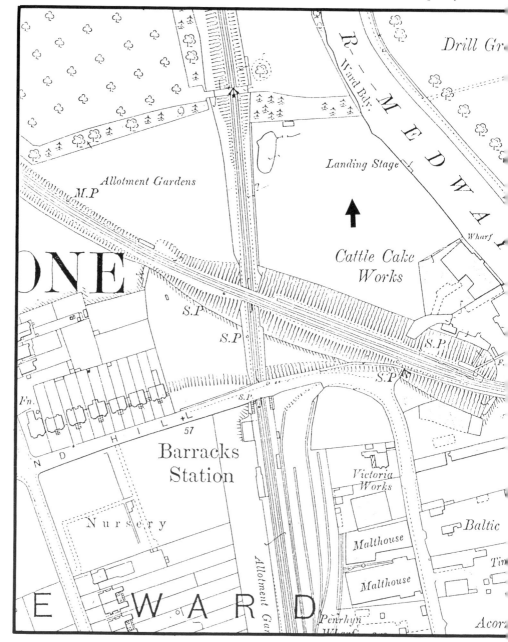

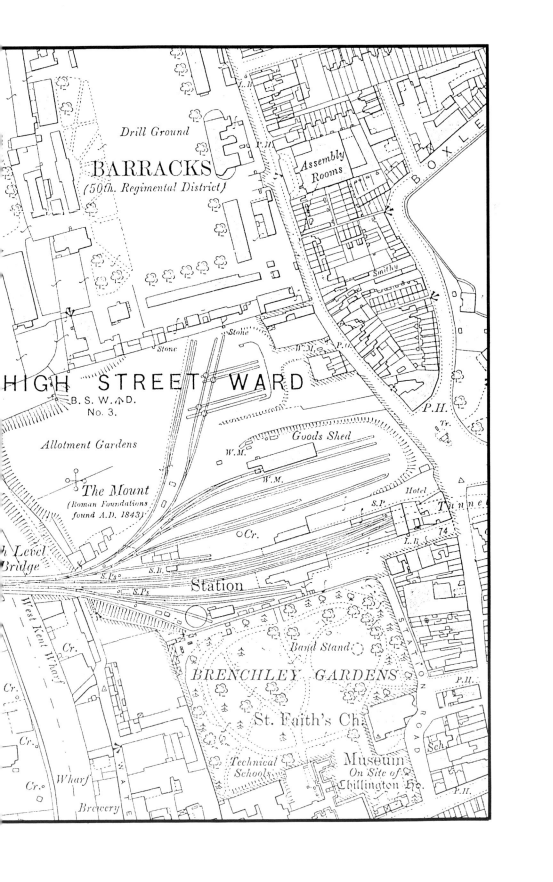

Drill Ground

BARRACKS
(50th. Regimental District)

Assembly Rooms

P.H.

Smithy

Stone

Stone

Stone

W.M. *P.O.*

HIGH STREET WARD

B. S. W. & D.
No. 3.

P.H.

Tr.

Allotment Gardens

W.M. *Goods Shed*

W.M.

The Mount
(Roman Foundations found A.D. 1843)

Hotel

S.P. *Tunnel*

Cr.

L.B. 74

h Level
Bridge

S.Ps. *S.B.*

S.Ps. **Station**

West Kent Wharf

Cr.

Band Stand

Cr.

BRENCHLEY GARDENS

P.H.

Cr.

St. Faith's Ch.

STATION ROAD

Sch.

Cr. Wharf

Technical Schools

Museum
On Site of
Chillington Ho.

P.H.

Brewery

70. On the approach to the Medway bridge our route passes over the former SER Medway Valley line north of Maidstone Barracks station. This northward view from the 1930s includes class E no. 1491 bound for London and the Maidstone Corporation siding, which was mentioned but not illustrated in our *Strood to Paddock Wood* album. (S.A.Osborne)

71. An upstream view shows the bow-string original bridge, corn mills on the right and a brewery in the distance. The 113ft long span presented a weight restriction for locomotives and was replaced in 1927. (Kent Arts & Libraries Ashrail Collection)

72. The 1927 "High Level" bridge was photographed from its west end soon after completion. A footpath (right) was incorporated, which gives pedestrian access between East and Barracks stations. The signal box and down platform are in the distance. (Kent Arts & Libraries Ashrail Collection)

73. Class M3 4-4-0 no. 476 stands in the up bay alongside class D 4-4-0 no. 477 displaying SECR headcodes. Week Street tunnel is to the right of the brazier. The signal box was replaced by a modern structure nearby on 8th April 1962. It has controlled the line between Kemsing and Hothfield since 1984. (Lens of Sutton)

74. A westward view in June 1923 includes a "Birdcage" three-coach set in the centre road and a breakdown crane near the up bay. Milk churns were a feature of most stations at that time. (H.J.Patterson Rutherford)

75. Class F1 no. 1233 heads a line of locomotives resting between duties in the late afternoon of 3rd December 1932. The coach is standing in the up bay and the white-lined turntable pit is on the right, as is the engine shed. The shed then was allocated eight locomotives of this class and closed in 1933. (H.C.Casserley)

76. The early up side building is also seen in the left background of picture no. 74. Lower left is the buffer-stop lamp of the up bay platform. (D.Cullum coll.)

77. Following the closure of the building seen in the previous picture, a booking hall was provided above the tracks, together with covered ramps shown in this and the next picture. From 1939 until 1961, conductor rail continued a short way into the tunnel for shunting purposes. (Lens of Sutton)

78.   This and the next picture were taken on 4th August 1951. Class 4P LMS-designed no. 42094 is about to depart for Ashford with an assortment of ex-SR coaches. The centre berthing road was resignalled in 1961 for reversible running by passenger trains. (D.Cullum)

79.   No. 34089 *602 Squadron* has most of its train on High Level Bridge and is approaching the railings which protect the outer end of the down bay platform. On the right is the mill seen in picture no. 71. (D.Cullum)

80. Diesel no. D5013 takes water for its train steam heating boiler as it waits with the 11.3am from Ashford on 12th April 1961. Also included is the electrified up berthing siding and the premises of the famous commercial vehicle builder. (S.C.Nash)

81. The 14.08 Ashford to Victoria waits at platform 1 on 7th September 1989. The up bay had long gone and the down bay had become platform 3. This was rebuilt further north in 1994, greatly extended and redesignated "up bay". Most of the old buildings were still extant. (J.Scrace)

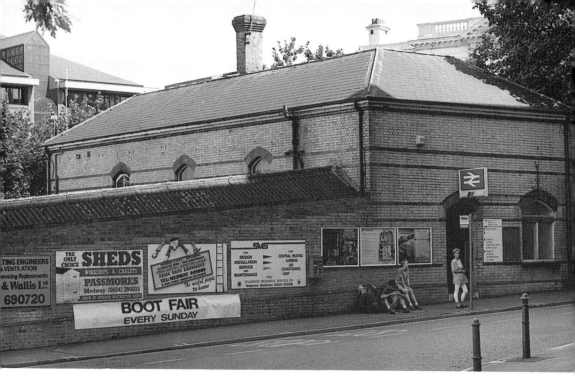

82.   The imposing County Hall is in the background of the previous picture but the station does not warrant comparison with it. The entrance to the booking hall is on the side of the building in a side street. (J.Scrace)

83.   This and the previous photograph were taken in August 1993 after the completion of track alterations which would allow international trains to use the centre road in either direction to pass 12-coach trains standing in both through platforms. New facing crossovers were provided each side of the station to facilitate such working. (J.Scrace)

84. At 02.12 on 6th September 1993 much of the new work was destroyed when no. 47288 with a train loaded with steel coils derailed at an estimated 60 mph on the 10 chain curve which was subject to a 25 mph limit. As in the case of the destruction of Tattenham Corner station nine months earlier, the driver was drunk. (B.Morrison)

L.C. & D.R.
HOLLINGBOURNE
TO (8. 8)
MAIDSTONE.
THIRD CLASS
5d. 5d.
Available on the day of Issue only
See Other Side
MAIDSTONE MAIDSTONE
7924 7924

S. E. & C R SEE BACK.
Available Day of Issue ONLY.
MAIDSTONE EAST to
BEARSTED & THURNHAM
6d First Class 6d
BEARSTED & T. BEARSTED & T.
1214 1214

West of the station, about half a mile beyond the tunnels, is Turkey Mill Viaduct of seven brick arches and 210 ft length, which for many years was something of a curiosity. The nearby paper mill specialised in the manufacture of high-quality drawing paper, and to protect it from soot and sparks from locomotives, the railway was screened by a solid brick wall on the up side, and covered by a slated roof on an iron framework. On the down side, which was furthest from the mill, the screen-wall was perforated with openings for ventilation. In 1951, BR obtained powers to remove the roof and lower the screen-walls, and this work was carried out in 1953.

BEARSTED

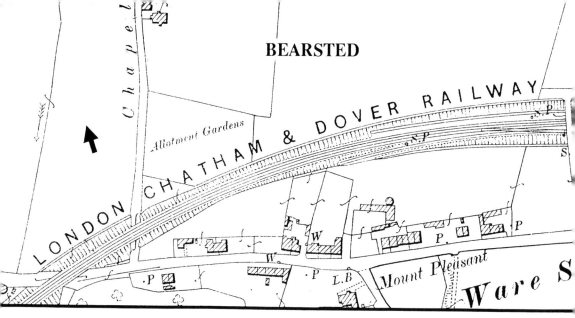

The 1897 survey shows the layout at its optimum. The nearby village housed under 700 when the line opened.

85.   The down refuge siding is in front of the signal box and behind it is a sandpit which was probably worked during the construction of the line in 1883-84. The crane is visible, it having a capacity of 30cwt. The goods shed was still standing in 1994. (Lens of Sutton)

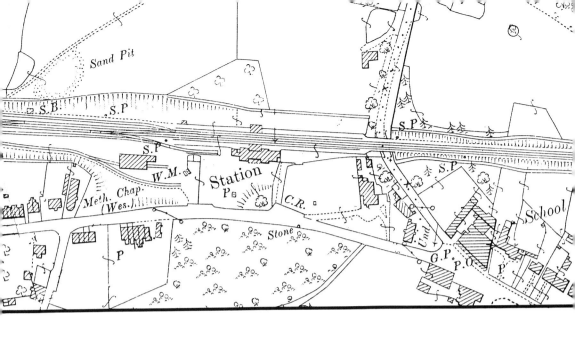

86. A down goods rattles off down the 1 in 100 gradient which will demand some skill in the brake van. This undated picture is post-World War II, evidenced by white bands on all vertical objects, a blackout precaution. (D.Cullum coll.)

87. BR class 2 2-6-2T no. 84024 accelerates a local train towards Maidstone East in September 1958. Flat bottom rail had arrived by then, except for the sidings. (P.Hay)

88. Passing Bearsted on 12th April 1961 are ex-LSWR class T9 no. 30117 and ex-SECR class D1 no. 31749 with an enthusiasts' railtour. The conductor rails would be in regular use six months later. (S.C.Nash)

89. This and the next picture record the scene in August 1989. The concrete footbridge arrived just prior to electrification and the goods yard closed on 7th October 1968. A new siding at Hollingworth (near Turkey Mill Viaduct) was brought into use on 31st March 1957 and was controlled electrically from Bearsted signal box, which closed on 14th April 1984. (J.Scrace)

90. The two-tone brickwork gives a pleasing effect to the south elevation of the station which was officially "Bearsted and Thurnham" from 1st July 1907 until 12th May 1980. To reduce the problems of leaves on the rails, a water spray system was installed experimentally here in 1978, jets of spring water acting for one minute in every eighteen. (J.Scrace)

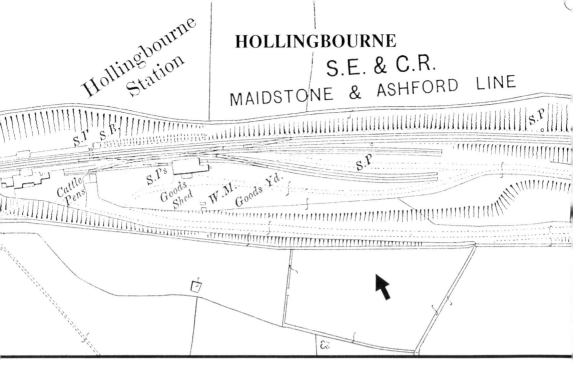

The 1909 map does not include the brick
and tile works south of the station. This would
have generated some coal traffic.

91. A view towards Maidstone shows three
lower quadrant signals and the usual dock
siding with cattle pen and end-loading
facilities for farm machinery and the like.
(Lens of Sutton)

92. A look in the other direction includes the barrow crossing and the loading gauge which was used before despatch of hay, timber and other bulky commodities. BR class 2 2-6-2T no. 84022 is working the Ashford-Maidstone East local service in September 1958. (P.Hay)

The 1906 timetable shows two trains terminating at Bearsted.

LONDON, SWANLEY, OTFORD, SEVENOAKS, MALLING, MAIDSTONE EAST, and ASHFORD.—S. E. & C.

Down.

Station								
Victoria..........dep.								
Holborn Viaduct ″								
St. Paul's ″								
Herne Hill ″								
Swanley ″								
Eynsford ″								
Shoreham (Kent) ″								
Otford Junction ″								
Otford Junc. ....dep.								
Seven- ⎰ Bat & Ball ″								
oaks ⎱ Tub's Hill ″								
Kemsing .... ″								
Wrotham and Borough ″								
Malling .... ″								
Barming .... ″								
Maidstone East........ ″								
Bearsted .... ″								
Hollingbourne............ ″								
Harrietsham............ ″								
Lenham .... ″								
Charing .... ″								
Hothfield .... ″								
Ashford 202, 215 arr.								

Up.

Mls	Station								
—	Ashford ....dep.								
5	Hothfield .... ″								
5¾	Charing .... ″								
9¼	Lenham .... ″								
11½	Harrietsham............ ″								
13¼	Hollingbourne............ ″								
16	Bearsted .... ″								
18½	Maidstone East........ ″								
21¾	Barming .... ″								
24	Malling ....[Green] ″								
29	Wrotham and Borough ″								
31½	Kemsing .... ″								
—	Sevenoaks (Tub's H.) ″								
—	″ (Bat & Ball) ″								
—	Otford Junc. ....arr.								
36½	Otford Junction........ ″								
37½	Shoreham (Kent) ...... ″								
40	Eynsford .... ″								
42½	Swanley 203 ....arr. ″								
56½	Herne Hill .... ″								
60	St. Paul's .... ″								
60	Holborn Viaduct ...... ″								
60½	Victoria............ ″								

93.   Three pictures from August 1989 reveal that most of the original features survived over 100 years after their erection. As elsewhere the footbridge was built prior to conductor rail energisation. (J.Scrace)

SOUTHERN RAILWAY.
Issued subject to the Bye-laws, Regulations & Conditions in the Company's Bills and Notices.
Hollingbourne to
Hollingbourne / Maidstone East
Hollingbourne / Maidstone East
MAIDSTONE EAST
THIRD CLASS   THIRD CLASS
Fare 9½d.   Fare 9½d.
NOT TRANSFERABLE.
1275   1275

94.   While Bearsted's population increased, Hollingbourne's decreased from 964 in 1891 to 754 in 1921. The former attracted some business travel while the latter suffered rural depopulation, so common for many decades. Commuters are now more numerous at this location. (J.Scrace)

95.   The main changes were the closure of the goods yard on 15th May 1961 (replaced by woodland) and the signal box on 14th April 1984. The train is the 13.39 Ashford to Victoria on 8th August 1989. (J.Scrace)

HARRIETSHAM

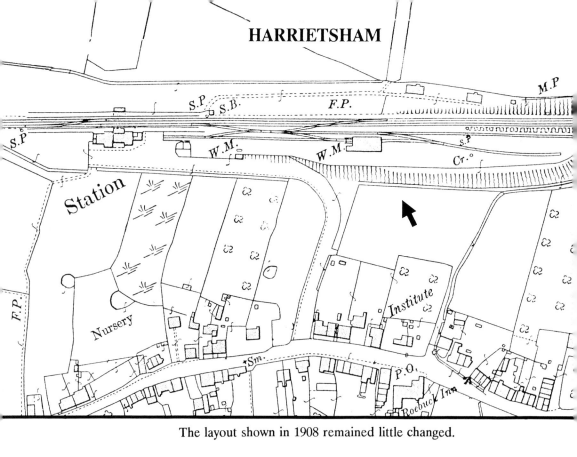

The layout shown in 1908 remained little changed.

96.   As the Maidstone-Ashford section opened as double track, the up and down buildings are in similar style at each station. Some conductor rail has been delivered, suggesting a photograph date of the summer of 1960. (Lens of Sutton)

97. The rear coach of this Maidstone East to Ashford train is near the summit of the 1 in 80 climb. The locomotive in this September 1958 view is BR class 2 no. 84022. (P.Hay)

98. Unit no. 3206 is seen working the 12.39 Ashford to Victoria on 8th August 1989. The closure of the goods yard had taken place on 1st May 1961 and that of the signal box followed on 5th November 1972. (J.Scrace)

99. The station served about 700 souls for its first 50 years. This timeless scene was recorded in 1989 in perfect weather. In 1994 the goods shed was still standing and the station windows were boarded up, although the booking office was still in use in the mornings. (J.Scrace)

S. E. & C. R.   'SEE BACK
Available Day of issue ONLY.

Harrietsham to

MAIDSTONE East

9d   Second Class   9d
Maidstone East   Maidstone East

2696   2696

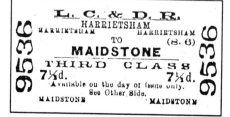

L. C. & D. R.
HARRIETSHAM
HARRIETSHAM   HARRIETSHAM
TO   (S. 6)
MAIDSTONE
THIRD   CLASS
7½d.   7½d.
Available on the day of issue only.
See Other Side.
MAIDSTONE   MAIDSTONE

9536   9536

100. On the left of this photograph and the map is the Morello Cherry Works which had access to the siding on the left. No. 84023 is hauling three coaches in "blood and custard" livery towards Maidstone East on 15th June 1958. For many years, pigs arrived by rail at the siding adjacent to Clarke's Bacon Factory. (P.Hay)

LENHAM

Lenham Station

S.P

S.P

S.B   S.P

S.P

S.P   P

S.P

S.P

Crane   W.M.

Goods Shed   W.M.

1909

101.   Electro-diesel no. 73205 *London Chamber of Commerce* conveys the Venice Simplon Orient Express coaches from Victoria to Folkestone Harbour on 7th September 1989. An electrified loop was laid through the goods yard in 1961. The yard closed on 6th January 1969. The down siding was converted into a loop and electrified in 1961. The goods office (left) was still standing in 1994. (J.Scrace)

102.   The stone springers for the window arches gave all the stations on the 1884 part of the route a controversial feature. One hundred years later most of the building was in commercial use but a semaphore signal could still be seen. (C.Hall)

103. A 1989 photograph shows the platform buildings to be complete. The signal box was replaced on 23rd July 1961, the new flat-roofed one being built adjacent to the original. It controlled both loops and was made redundant on 28th May 1984. It had light blue exterior panels. (J.Scrace)

104. Eurostar UK1, with power car no. 3101 leading, speeds east on 14th January 1994 on a test run from North Pole International Depot to Dollands Moor. Owing to its numerous speed restrictions, this route will continue to be second choice for expresses to the coast. A restricted public service commenced on 14th November 1994 through the Channel Tunnel from Waterloo to Paris and to Brussels. (C.Wilson)

CHARING

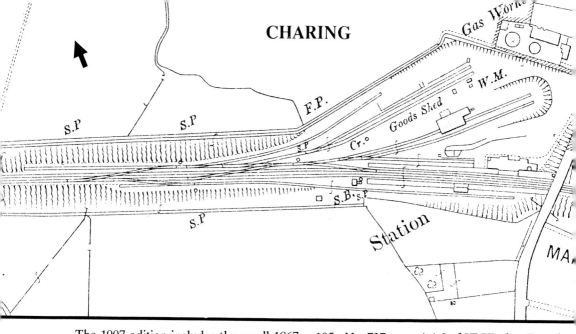

The 1907 edition includes the small 1867 gasworks which by 1914 supplied only 100 customers and 15 street lights, consuming 345 tons of coal; i.e. 35 loaded wagons per annum. It was still in use in 1947. The upper siding was later designated for military use.

105. No. 737 was a 4-4-0 of SECR class D and was built at Ashford in 1901 and is now a prized exhibit at the National Railway Museum. Sadly the details concerning the special train were not recorded but the goods yard can be studied. (British Rail)

106. Goods facilities were withdrawn on 16th May 1964 but the signal box remained open until 14th April 1984. The nearby village had about 1200 residents during the first 50 years of the railway. (Lens of Sutton)

107. The hourly train from Ashford arrives in September 1958. All the platform buildings remained in use, little changed, in the 1990s and so are not illustrated further. (P.Hay)

HOTHFIELD HALT

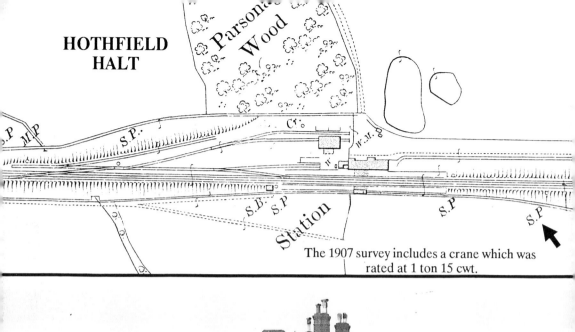

The 1907 survey includes a crane which was rated at 1 ton 15 cwt.

108. As with the other stations east of Maidstone, this had identical architectural details and opened with the line. It was the least successful and became a halt when it lost its platform staff on 25th September 1937. (Lens of Sutton)

109. The signal box was staffed until 28th April 1984 but was retained as a ground frame until 16th February 1985. (Lens of Sutton)

110. Freight facilities were retained until 22nd February 1964 but passenger services were withdrawn on 2nd November 1959. The platforms would have required substantial increase in height and length. (Lens of Sutton)

111. Military sidings were in use on the south side of the line during World War II. Sidings were provided in 1979 on the north side for the reception of roadstone at Tarmac's depot. They were extended in 1986 and receive approximately 300,000 tonnes annually from quarries in Somerset and Leicestershire. There are two coated roadstone plants and an aggregate store.
(Tarmac Roadstone (Southern) Ltd.)

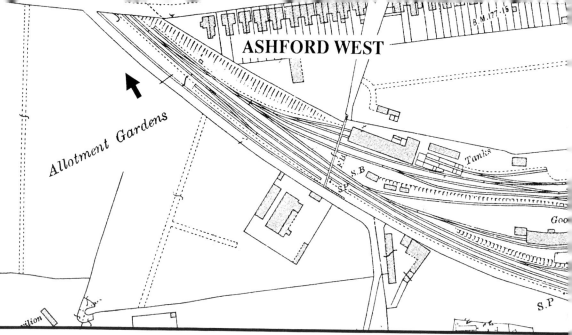

The 1933 map marks the LCDR terminus as disused. This had been the case since 1st January 1899 after which date all trains ran into the ex-SER station which is just off the right border of the map. The line from Maidstone East is top left and this was first connected to the SER tracks here on 1st November 1891.

112. This is the only photograph known to exist of the LCDR terminus in use. The platform canopies were still standing in the mid-1930s although the lines had been mainly used for storage of cattle wagons. The turntable went to Deal in 1904. (Lens of Sutton)

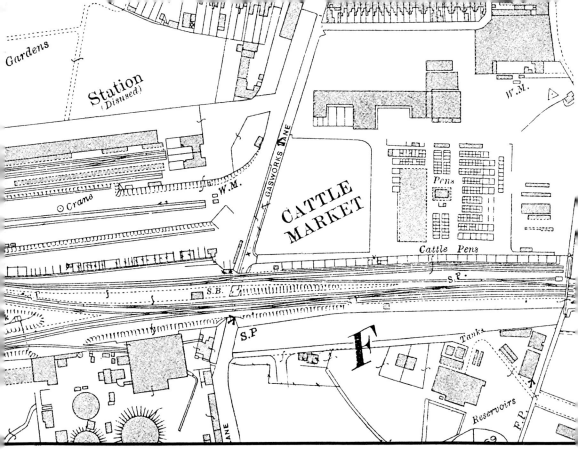

113. This and the next four photographs were taken on 18th July 1957 to record the remains of the once extensive terminus which served principally as the town's goods depot after 1899. The wagons on the left are standing on the lines shown in the previous picture. (A.E.Bennett)

114. A more substantial version of the other 1884 buildings, the terminus became railway offices and was still standing in 1994, partly used for residential purposes. (A.E.Bennett)

115. The former LCDR engine shed and "A" Box are marked on the left of the map. The box was reduced to ground frame status on 22nd December 1929 after which date "B" Box at the junction controlled access to the yard by means of another ground frame. (A.E.Bennett)

116. The engine shed and adjacent buildings were converted to an engine sponge-cloth works. Here more than a million engine cleaning cloths were processed annually, the dirty oil being extracted by means of steam for reuse on points and the like. The cloths were returned to locomotive depots for reuse. (A.E.Bennett)

117. The LCDR carriage shed was used for storage purposes, although its east end was roofless. This is evident on the left of pictures 113 and 114. Cattle wagons were once in demand here. In 1932 69244 animals were loaded at the long cattle market siding shown on the map. On one day, 220 trucks of sheep were despatched in five trains. (A.E.Bennett)

118. The 36-lever "C" Box controlled the west end of the station, visible through the bridge arches. Both were extensively rebuilt in 1958-

61. No. 42095 accelerates the 5.0pm departure for Maidstone East towards the junction on 20th June 1954. (N.W.Sprinks)

120. The train seen in picture no. 104 winds its 18 coaches round the junction curve, arcing severely. Eurostars can draw up to 1400 amps on the low voltage of 750 from the conductor rails and cause problems. Ashford was building its own international station for opening in 1995 but sadly its railway heritage would receive little recognition. Unlike the daily press and TV, we heartily congratulate those who created this fine train and the country's greatest engineering and logistic achievement under the English Channel. (C.Wilson)

119. With snowploughs ready for the winter, no. 33054 squeals round the curve north of the junction on 30th August 1985, hauling wagons from the train ferry at Dover. In the background is the former LCDR goods shed. A long electrified down loop was added from here almost to the station in 1994. (J.S.Petley)

> **Ashford Works and the evolution of Ashford's other station from SER to BR are illustrated in the companion albums** *Hastings to Ashford, Ashford to Dover, Redhill to Ashford* **and** *Branch Lines around Canterbury.*
> *(The latter is due mid-1995).*

MP Middleton Press

Easebourne Lane, Midhurst. West Sussex. GU29 9AZ   Tel: (0730) 813169 Fax: (0730) 812601
. . . . . Write or telephone for our latest list . . . . .

BRANCH LINES

Branch Line to Allhallows
Branch Lines to Alton
Branch Lines tround Ascot
Branch Line to Bude
Branch Lines to East Grinstead
Branch Lines tround Effingham Jn
Branch Lines to Exmouth
Branch Line to Fairford
Branch Lines around Gosport
Branch Line to Hawkhurst
Branch Line to Hayling
Branch Lines to Horsham
Branch Lines around Huntingdon
Branch Lines to Ilfracombe
Branch Lines to Longmoor
Branch Line to Lyme Regis
Branch Line to Lynton
Branch Lines around March
Branch Lines around Midhurst
Branch Line to Minehead
Branch Lines to Newport
Branch Lines around Portmadoc 1923-46
Branch Lines around Porthmadog 1954-94
Branch Lines to Seaton & Sidmouth
Branch Line to Selsey
Branch Lines around Sheerness
Branch Line to Shrewsbury
Branch Line to Southwold
Branch Line to Swanage
Branch Line to Tenterden
Branch Lines to Torrington
Branch Lines to Tunbridge Wells
Branch Lines tround Weymouth
Branch Lines around Wimborne

LONDON SUBURBAN RAILWAYS

Caterham and Tattenham Corner
Charing Cross to Dartford
Crystal Palace and Catford Loop
Holborn Viaduct to Lewisham
Kingston and Hounslow Loops
Lewisham to Dartford
London Bridge to Addiscombe
Mitcham Junction Lines
West Croydon to Epsom

STEAMING THROUGH

Steaming through Cornwall
Steaming through East Sussex
Steaming through the Isle of Wight
Steaming through Surrey
Steaming through West Hants
Steaming through West Sussex

SOUTH COAST RAILWAYS

Ashford to Dover
Bournemouth to Weymouth
Brighton to Eastbourne
Brighton to Worthing
Chichester to Portsmouth
Dover to Ramsgate
Eastbourne to Hastings
Hastings to Ashford
Ryde to Ventnor
Southampton to Bournemouth

SOUTHERN MAIN LINES

Basingstoke to Salisbury
Bromley South to Rochester
Charing Cross to Orpington
Crawley to Littlehampton
Dartford to Sittingbourne
East Croydon to Three Bridges
Epsom to Horsham
Exeter to Barnstaple
Faversham to Dover
Haywards Heath to Seaford
London Bridge to East Croydon
Orpington to Tonbridge
Salisbury to Yeovil
Sittingbourne to Ramsgate
Three Bridges to Brighton
Tonbridge to Hastings
Victoria to Bromley South
Waterloo to Windsor
Waterloo to Woking
Woking to Southampton
Yeovil to Exeter

COUNTRY RAILWAY ROUTES

Andover to Southampton
Bath To Evercreech Junction
Bournemouth to Evercreech Jn
Burnham to Evercreech Junction
East Kent Light Railway
Fareham to Salisbury
Guildford to Redhill
Reading to Basingstoke
Reading to Guildford
Redhill to Ashford
Strood to Paddock Wood
Woking to Alton

SOUTHERN RAILWAY VIDEO

War on the Line

TRAMWAY CLASSICS

Brighton's Tramways
Camberwell & W. Norwood Tramw
Dover's Tramways
Exeter & Taunton Tramways
Greenwich & Dartford Tramway
Hastings Tramways
Lewisham & Catford Tramways
Maidstone & Chatham
Southampton Tramways
Southend-on-sea Tramways
Thanet's Tramways

BUS BOOKS

Eastbourne Bus Story
Tillingbourne Bus Story

OTHER RAILWAY BOOKS

Garraway Father & Son
Industrial Railways of the South E
London Chatham & Dover Railw
South Eastern Railway
War on the Line

MILITARY BOOKS

Battle Over Portsmouth
Battle Over Sussex 1940
Blitz Over Sussex 1941-42
Military Defence of West Sussex

WATERWAY ALBUMS

Hampshire Waterways
Kent and East Sussex Waterways
London to Portsmouth Waterwa
West Sussex Waterways

COUNTRY BOOKS

Brickmaking in Sussex
East Grinstead Then and Now
Leigh Park
Walking Ashdown Forest